The Connected Life
Small Groups That Create Community

THE CONNECTED LIFE

SMALL GROUPS THAT CREATE COMMUNITY

JACOB ARMSTRONG

WITH RACHEL ARMSTRONG

Abingdon Press / Nashville

The Connected Life
Small Groups That Create Community

This book is printed on elemental chlorine-free paper.
978-1-5018-4345-7

17 18 19 20 21 22 23 24 25 26 — 10 9 8 7 6 5 4 3 2 1

MANUFACTURED IN THE UNITED STATES OF AMERICA

CONTENTS

Introduction: Disconnected 7

1. Why Small Groups? 13

2. What Do Small Groups Do? 21

3. Forming Small Groups 33

4. The First Two Sessions 47

5. Overseeing Small Groups 55

Conclusion: The Connected Life 63

Appendix: Sample Forms 69

INTRODUCTION:
DISCONNECTED

Disconnected. So many of us feel it. Our lives are full but not connected. We are busy but feel disjointed.

We can feel disconnected from people. We can feel disconnected from our dreams and our purpose. We can feel disconnected from the church. We can feel disconnected from God.

Strangely, even though technology has given us many more ways of connecting, people now report higher levels of loneliness and despair than ever before. Anxiety runs rampant; depression leaves us cold and dark.

I recently talked with a young businessman in our community. By most standards he was successful. He had quickly moved up the ladder in the real estate business. We were meeting to discuss a new position he had been offered by another, more prominent company. His finances were secure. His wife seemed happy. His children went to a good school. He volunteered in the community and served on several leadership teams in the church.

"I'm miserable," he said.

For the first time I really looked into his eyes, and I saw it. He was exhausted. He was lonely. He was afraid. With all that he had going on, he felt he was going nowhere. He interacted with lots of people every day, but he rarely connected with anyone. Ironically, this person known in our community as a well-connected guy was actually experiencing feelings of great disconnection.

For that young man, for you, for all of us, I have good news! Jesus was all about connecting the disconnected. He was constantly looking to those who were on the outside—the hurting, but also the busy and the religious. Jesus drew people to him with intriguing teaching and amazing miracles, but his goal wasn't to draw a crowd. He wanted to connect people to people. He wanted to connect people to God.

Notice that after Jesus would teach, draw a crowd, or work a miracle, he often would lead people to a meal, or a boat, or a conversation with a smaller group. The parables were discussed in small circles of followers. The miracles were marveled over when twelve got on a boat together. There, away from the noise of the crowd and the trappings of religious institutions, people were connected to Jesus in a deeper way. At the same time, they were connected to each other.

Jesus invites us to do the same thing. He leads us out of disconnection and into the connected life. He wants to gather his followers in living rooms and around dinner tables. He wants us to give more space and time to others and to God, and usually this takes place with a smaller group of people. In the connected life we begin to find purpose in movement, in busy-ness, even in brokenness.

If you look at Jesus' travels on a map, you will see that his three-year public ministry appears haphazard, like a child's connect-the-dots activity gone wrong. There seems to be no pattern or linear progress from one place to the next. How many times did he cross that lake only to go back to the other side again?

Jesus' travels, like our lives, were not from point A to point B. He knew that connection is found not in where we are going but with whom we journey. For that reason, the connected life is experienced in the midst of movement. We can find it in rush-hour traffic or in a soccer mom's minivan, in a cubicle or in retirement.

The connected life is first found by connecting with Jesus.

Jesus said, "I am the vine; you are the branches. If you remain in me and I in you, you will bear much fruit; apart from me, you can do nothing" (John 15:5).

Oh, how we try to do so many things apart from Jesus! We try and we try and we come up wanting. The truth is, without Jesus we can't do anything. But in Jesus, remaining in him, connecting with him, we can do all things.

My guess is if you have picked up this book, you have sought an intentional connection with Jesus, and you have probably tried to connect others with him. Don't forget, though, that even as we seek to connect others, we must ourselves abide in Jesus, remembering always that we are branches and our source of life is the vine.

The connected life is also found in connecting with others—on the porch, at a picnic table, on a boat going across the water once again. It's about living a different way, and it will require great intentionality in meeting with people—the same people, in the same rhythm, over a period of time.

Whether you call it a small group, a life group, a connect group, or a Sunday school class, I believe that the key to connection and purpose is found in journeying through life with these people.

In this book I will tell you the story of how one church formed small groups, only to find that the small groups were what formed the church. I will share how small groups became the reason people were coming back to church. I will share how the groups were not a ministry of the church but the place where ministry happened. In these small groups, congregational care, outreach, and evangelism happened in a natural, well-connected way. I will share the mistakes we made, the failures along the way, and the things we learned. I will share how you will have to figure much of this out on your own as you know your congregation and listen to your community. I will share how we have seen small groups change people's lives. I will share how miracles still happen. I will share how a group can journey through tragedy and grief. I will share how people have been saved by moving from a life of disconnection to a place of deep connection with God and others.

After sharing the reasons and results, I'll move to nuts and bolts. You'll read about how our church sets up small groups—the who, what, where, when, and how. I'll lay out our format for the first two sessions and the sessions that follow. I'll describe some of the very practical ways that we oversee our small group ministry in an ongoing way. None of these ideas are written in stone, even for us. They are simply suggestions. You'll want to consider them, take a look at your church, and adapt the ideas as needed for your own setting.

Remember the young real estate agent I mentioned earlier? Shortly after our meeting, he joined a small group. Five young couples just starting their families and careers began to meet in their living rooms twice a month for a time of food, fellowship, study, and prayer. Those regular meetings became a part of the rhythm of their lives. The young man found connection, accountability, and, in a real way, life. He began to teach and found areas of service in the church that were more connected to his gifts and passions. Light began to pierce through the darkness—not a one-time blinding light, but slow steady streams of light as he journeyed to a more connected life with a small group of people.

That is my hope for you as you take on the difficult but beautiful task of finding connection. Not that you would create just another church program; most of us already have plenty of those! But that you would prayerfully work to form a strategy and structure that allow people to do what they were created to do—to connect with God and connect with each other.

1

WHY SMALL GROUPS?

1

WHY SMALL GROUPS?

For me, it all started in Mexico. Monterrey, Mexico, to be exact. My wife, Rachel, and I felt called to be missionaries, and after many months of discernment found ourselves in Monterrey being introduced to our new neighbors and partners in ministry. We saw where we would live and where our girls would go to school. We dreamed about what God could do in the city. Honestly, we wondered where two unequipped but willing Jesus followers would fit into the mix, but in spite of that we were excited God had called us.

Then it all fell apart. All the things that needed to happen didn't happen. Perhaps you've experienced this. You thought you knew where God was leading, where your life was going, but it turned out that what needed to happen didn't happen. That's where we found ourselves.

Confused, disappointed, and disconnected.

As we sorted through our feelings, we found God leading us down a new path. Only a few months after the big no in Mexico, we began hearing a big yes from God regarding another opportunity. Instead of traveling thousands of miles away, we were invited to start a new church in our hometown—Mt. Juliet, Tennessee.

Coming Home

We moved back home knowing almost nothing about starting a new church. What we had, though, was a strong sense of calling to help those who feel disconnected from God and the church to find hope, healing, and wholeness in Jesus Christ.

A few months into starting Providence Church, we had a few dozen people who were on board with the vision God had given us. That vision, which had grown out of our experience as failed missionaries, seemed to resonate with many in our community.

I had assumed that my main task in starting a new church would be to create a weekly worship service, but surprisingly those thirty or forty people were not hungering for weekly worship; instead they wanted connection They were longing, whether they realized it or not, for some other people to join them on their life journey. They wanted to do life in a disciplined rhythm with others who, like themselves, were seeking meaning and purpose. They wanted to learn about Jesus, to grow in their faith, maybe even to be the church.

We didn't really know how to do any of that, but we learned quickly that it wouldn't happen in isolation. It wouldn't be accomplished just by worshiping together on Sunday mornings. Worship would be central to the life of our church, but small groups would become its lifeblood, and they remain so today. They would be the place where faith was nurtured, growth was achieved, and people found connection.

We started groups out of necessity. We were missing something big without them. People were longing for connection, and my guess is you will start yours for the same reason. You may already have small groups and are looking for a new model. You may be a new church and are looking for a way to make and grow disciples. You may be an established church with Sunday school or programmatic classes during the week. For those of you who already have a strong Sunday school, you may simply consider how some of the principles laid out here can fit into what you already do well. Whatever your setting, you still see the need for the regular gathering of smaller groups together in circles, not rows. Something happens in that setting that doesn't happen anywhere else, and what happens is biblical.

Pentecost: The Rest of the Story

As a pastor starting a new church, I spent a lot of time reading the Acts of the Apostles. This fifth book in the New Testament takes us from the four accounts of the life of Jesus to what happened after Jesus ascended to heaven. Acts records the story of Jesus' first followers, who were trying to figure out what it meant to be the church. In Acts 2, we get Luke's account of the actual birth of the church. It's a pretty crazy story!

You may be familiar with the story of Pentecost. The followers of Jesus were gathered together. They were waiting. That's what Jesus had told them to do. He told them to wait in Jerusalem for the Holy Spirit. But he didn't tell them when the Holy Spirit would arrive or what the Holy Spirit's arrival would look like. They just waited. It's possible there was some confusion, disappointment, maybe even feelings of disconnection among those first followers. After all, they had just gone from walking with Jesus to hiding out in locked rooms. They were waiting for the Holy Spirit, but when? and how?

Well, when the Holy Spirit came it was like nothing they had imagined. There was the sound of a violent wind, there was visible fire hovering over people's heads, and to top it all off they began speaking in different languages. That's how the church started!

It caused such a commotion that it attracted Jews who had come to Jerusalem from around the world for the Feast of Pentecost. They were drawn to the strange thing happening with the ragtag followers of this Jesus of Nazareth, who by the way was nowhere to be found. Some of them accused the Jesus followers of being drunk.

Others were intrigued to hear the followers speaking in their native language.

Peter, seizing the moment, explained that what the Jews were witnessing had actually been predicted centuries before through the prophet Joel. Peter said this was what Joel had meant when he said,

> "'In the last day, God says,
>> I will pour out my Spirit on all people.
> Your sons and daughters will prophesy,
>> Your young men will see visions,
>> Your old men will dream dreams.
> Even on my servants, both men and women,
>> I will pour out my Spirit in those days,
>> and they will prophesy.'"

(Acts 2:17-18)

After Peter placed the events of Pentecost in the context of their historic faith, he began telling the Jews about Jesus. They had all heard about the miracle-working teacher who had recently died a criminal's death on a cross; now Peter told them the hard-to-believe news that after three days Jesus had risen from the grave and was indeed the Messiah they had been waiting for. What they were witnessing now was the promised Spirit that both Joel and Jesus had said was coming. In response, the people asked what they should do next. Peter said, "Repent and be baptized."

That day, three thousand were added to the small number of Jesus followers. Three thousand. It was the birth of the church.

The Plan

We don't know how the disciples decided what to do next. We don't know how many meetings they had or what discussion ensued. We don't know if they disseminated a handbook (OK, probably not). We don't know where or how the plan for the church was drawn up, but we do know what the plan was, because it's described in Acts.

Usually when reading the Scripture on Pentecost Sunday, we stop at Acts 2:41, which says three thousand were added to their number. But verse 42 is where the blueprint for the church begins to unfold. We are told what the first church of Christians did as a practice. Are you ready for it?

Acts 2:42 says, "They started worshiping for one hour on Sunday mornings."

Actually, no! That's not what it says at all. Weekly worship—what has become for us the main thing we think of as church—clearly came later.

Acts 2.42 really says, "They devoted themselves to the apostles' teaching and to fellowship, to the breaking of bread and to prayer."

There's more: Verses 43-45 tell us God performed many wonders and signs, and the believers shared their possessions, sold their property, and gave the proceeds to those in need. Verse 46 says they met together regularly and shared bread in their homes, and this practice gave them glad and sincere hearts! Verse 47 says they praised God and every day saw God add people to the number who were being saved.

Like me, you may have been more familiar with the story of the church's birth than the description of how the church operated in its first season. As the pastor of a new church, I was intrigued by the power of the Holy Spirit in the early church, the miracles that were worked, and the way the people gathered together.

After a few months of trying to start a new church, before we began weekly worship, we started our first small groups. We started two. These two groups pretty much involved all the adults who were part of our first gatherings. These two groups are still meeting today, some nine years later. During that time a lot has changed in the life of the groups and the makeup of the groups, but they continue the rhythm that they started. The groups use Acts 2:42 as the model for how they gather and associate, just as do the dozens and dozens of additional groups we have started since then.

So, why small groups? When Jesus followers come together in common life and common worship, there will be a natural hunger for a regular gathering of smaller groups. Acts 2 shows us that when the Spirit comes alive in God's people, they experience salvation, power, and miracles.

We gather in large groups to worship God and hear the Word proclaimed. And then, like the early believers, we gather in small groups to share meals, to study, to pray, and to connect.

2

WHAT DO SMALL GROUPS DO?

2

WHAT DO SMALL GROUPS DO?

Small groups can meet in many different places and at many different times, and they can look very different. But we have found that four components are "nonnegotiable" in holding a group together:

- Devotion to the apostles' teaching
- Fellowship
- Breaking of bread
- Prayer

Core Activities

Most of our groups meet in homes for ninety minutes to two hours. We also have groups that meet in public places such as coffee shops and gyms, while still others meet at the church during the week. Our ideal group size is twelve to sixteen adults. Some of our groups meet every other week, while others meet weekly.

But wherever and whenever they meet, all the groups devote themselves to the apostles' teaching, fellowship, breaking of bread, and prayer.

Devotion to the Apostles' Teaching

For our small groups, this means the study and application of the Bible. Our small groups have at their center a time when the Bible is read and discussed. It is a time for teaching, questions, and exploration.

In worship we read from our holy book, and usually a pastor or teacher shares a message based upon and related to the Scripture. This has been central to worship for hundreds and hundreds of years. Hearing Scripture in worship is only one way to encounter the holy book. Worship services do not usually allow for conversation, questions, or exploration. In a small group setting, though, we are allowed to go deeper. We hear different perspectives. We tell our stories and find application to life.

Small groups in the church should have time dedicated to the study of Scripture. Many of our small groups use a sermon discussion guide that we create each week to go along with the sermon. The guide gives other Scriptures and questions designed for a group discussion of forty-five minutes to an hour. This allows people to build on what is already happening in the life of the church. Of course, many other groups use Bible studies and small group curriculum that is approved and often provided by the church.

Small groups that study the Scriptures are able to frame their life stories around the story of God and God's people. This type of study does not require a seminary-trained teacher; it only requires people who are open to ways the Holy Spirit can guide and teach through the reading and application of the Bible.

Fellowship

The word fellowship, which comes from the Greek koinonia, is more easily experienced than explained. However, a good (but not complete) definition of koinonia is "joint participation." Fellowship is a way of jointly participating in life. A more recent phrase I have heard is "doing life together."

Fellowship is not just coming together for a Bible study; it is jointly participating or doing life together. It is sharing joys and sorrows. It is celebrating successes and being quiet in disappointment—together. The hard-to-explain but easy-to-experience fellowship is the thing that keeps you coming back to your small group. It's what makes you, after a hard day at work, feel pulled to go to your small group, when every logical impulse would say to stay home and sit on the couch. Fellowship is something that the Holy Spirit creates among believers that is not just participation in life; it gives life. How do you create fellowship? You pray for it, you dive into the Word, you gather around the table.

The fellowship experienced in a small group is different from the feeling in a business setting or even a church meeting. It is more akin to a family gathering. It involves light conversation and sharing of the deepest parts of your life. Fellowship is not something you can manufacture; but when it happens, you can't miss it.

Breaking of Bread

The phrase "breaking of bread" in Acts 2:42 probably referred in some way to the commemorative breaking of bread in Holy Communion. No doubt, the early home gatherings of the first Christians involved a remembrance of the Lord's Supper.

It is also reasonable, however, to think that sometimes the breaking of bread simply meant sharing a meal. We are told the early church shared everything in common, and even today one of the best things for believers to share in common is food.

So, the small groups at Providence Church involve food! For many groups this means eating a meal together. For other groups this is more difficult or not feasible, but in some way food is still involved, because it fosters fellowship.

Something happens with fried chicken that can't happen without it!

Prayer

Prayer is central to the church, and small groups provide an opportunity and a place for prayer that is not easily found in larger church gatherings. Small groups pray together and pray for each other.

In worship it's often difficult to find a good time or an appropriate way to pray for the needs of all those who attend. Oftentimes prayer in worship can go on too long or include details that are not appropriate for corporate sharing. We have also found that guests can feel excluded when insider requests are shared.

Small groups are a perfect place for personal concerns to be lifted up and prayed over. Prayer requests can easily be followed up and kept up in a small group. However, small groups are effective with more than just traditional prayer requests. Groups provide a place where people grow in their prayer life as the church is prayed for and God's spirit is invited. Groups are a place where people mature in their understanding of prayer and learn to be more comfortable praying. Some of their prayers take place in the heart and others are audible, though at Providence we make it clear that no one will be called upon to pray publicly if they haven't first expressed an interest in doing so.

*   *   *

We have found that when shared over time, these four components— the apostles' teaching, fellowship, breaking of bread, and prayer— create a small group that is life-giving both for individuals and for the church. When one of the four is neglected, the group suffers.

For instance, recently we learned of a group that over time had let their study of Scripture become less important, to the point that they weren't regularly having time for Bible study. They had fellowship, food, and prayer but were not having any facilitated time for Scripture.

When their small group coach (a role we'll discuss later) learned of this regular omission, she was able to help the group understand the importance of study, and they resumed their work with Scripture.

Conversely, another group simply gathered for Bible study and didn't focus on the other three components. In that group, and in similar groups over the years, the members have benefited from study, but we have found that prayer, food, and fellowship cause something much deeper to happen.

Small Groups Are Where Ministry Happens

We have found that groups following this four-part pattern become not a ministry of the church but a place where the ministry of the church happens. This is true with outreach, evangelism, and care.

Small Groups as Outreach

The outreach ministry of Providence Church flows through the small groups. Our outreach ministries connect with and employ small groups to be the volunteer force that make the ministry go. Small groups cook and serve food at our weekly Care Night, which reaches the hurting and hopeless in our community. Small groups fully run our ministries to the homeless. When we need servants for a particular project, we don't put out a signup sheet on Sunday; we reach out to our small groups.

Recently at one of our ministries to the homeless, a small group connected with a family that was living on the streets. The group was able to come alongside this family and support them through a process that led eventually to a fully furnished apartment and more permanent housing. Partly as a result, the family began participating at Providence.

Outreach and mission are a natural outgrowth of the activities described in Acts 2:42, whether practiced today or two thousand years ago. A small group that is praying, learning, and living life together will naturally begin to serve each other and those in the community.

Small Groups as Congregational Care

At Providence we don't view pastors as the only ones who can provide care when church members and attenders are in times of need. In fact, the small group does a much better job! It is the norm, not the exception, for a pastor to make a hospital visit only to be preceded by members of the small group.

The small group members are more closely connected and stay longer than any pastor would. They organize meals and make sure the lawn is mowed. They express care for each other at group sessions and then offer care for each other when problems arise.

I recently went to visit the home of a church member who had died that morning. It was a Sunday morning, and I had been at church. The family, though, was not alone. Members of their small group had been there when the young father of three passed away. They were there that afternoon when I left, and they have been present in the grief process and transition to a new way of life for the family.

Small Groups as Evangelism

It's fascinating and inspiring to me that some folks who don't feel comfortable in worship on Sunday mornings are more than happy to participate with a small group in the home of a friend or neighbor. Eating and talking in a living room can seem much more normal than what we do in worship!

At Providence we have multiple stories of people who joined small groups as nonbelievers and over time gave their lives to Christ, eventually being baptized and serving actively in the life of the church. One member of my own small group, a man with a brilliant scientific mind who works in a medical field, attended the group regularly for three years before confessing his belief in Christ. The small group gave him a safe place to listen, observe, ask questions, and finally commit.

The small group can become a place where church happens. It's why we say that our church was formed around small groups. Which leads to a question you may be wondering: "Why should we start small groups?"

Reasons to Try Small Groups

For one reason or another you picked up this book and have made it this far! Maybe you've heard about churches forming small groups and are curious to learn what it's all about. Maybe you're frustrated with your church's current way of gathering people for discipleship. Maybe you and others in your church long for a more personal experience.

There are many reasons to try small groups. Here are a few reasons you may recognize:

We no longer want to be clergy-centric.

For years the predominant model for pastors was to be a solo hero-leader. The pastor unlocked the church, preached, taught, visited, and cleaned the bathrooms. I'm exaggerating, but you get the point. A healthy small group ministry in your church can be a way of opening up the bottleneck that often happens around the pastor. Small groups enable the laity to receive care from each other. Small groups allow for discipleship to happen without a seminary-trained expert. Small groups empower each other to be the church.

We are looking for ways to help people go deeper.

Small groups provide a new way for people to grow in their relationships with each other and with Christ. Current models in your church may be stagnant; perhaps starting small groups can provide a new way for people to be part of intentional discipleship.

We want to help our people be invitational.

Small groups provide a way for your church members to be invitational and reach new people. People will be excited about their small group and want to invite friends and neighbors. People will be more inclined to invite folks to their home or to a gathering with food than to a church service. The small group can serve as a door for people to enter the life of the church. (Later, after the small group has become established, it may become less invitational, a problem we will discuss below.)

Our church is growing, and we need a way to connect those who are coming.

You may be experiencing growth in your church but may have noticed that folks are not connecting with the church outside of Sunday morning worship. You'll find, if you haven't already, that new people who don't connect will find the back door of the church as quickly as they found the front door. New small groups that are forming can feel more accessible than joining an existing class or group.

We are out of space!

You may not have physical space on Sunday mornings for groups to meet, or you may be a mobile church that shares or rents space. As I mentioned, our church started small groups out of necessity. We needed everyone to serve on Sunday mornings, setting up and tearing down a worship space at the school each week, and we didn't have rooms for groups to meet. We found, though, after forming small groups out of necessity, that we would never go back.

When we planned our first church building, small groups were no longer a necessity; now they were a matter of stewardship. Would we spend several million extra dollars to provide space for groups to meet, or would we make use of the spaces we already were using in our homes and businesses? We chose the Acts 2:42 model of staying in the home!

Context Is Everything

Yes, I strongly recommend trying small groups, but if you're looking for a cookie-cutter approach, you won't find it here! If we have learned anything at Providence, it's that there is no one formula for small group ministry. Context is everything.

Every situation is different; so each pastor and church leader must do the important work of listening and learning before starting anything new. Often we are excited about what we learned from a book or conference and hurry to implement it, without doing the difficult but critical work of listening to the people we serve. As a result, we may fail to learn from them what will work in our unique setting. Try listening. It's the fun part!

Having said that, I'm hoping it will still be helpful to give you some tried and true principles and best practices that we have learned; in fact, I believe there are many things in this book that will work if you try them. Equally important, though, will be time invested by you and your team in asking important questions and listening to the answers.

So many times I have met with pastors and church leaders who want to reach new people or provide new ministries but spend no time talking to those who would be affected. As a result, they end up with a new worship service at a time that doesn't work for the very people it's intended for; or they plan an outreach event that has no connection with anyone outside the church.

Now, many of you have already begun the work of listening. Perhaps this is what has led you to consider starting small groups. Maybe you've heard that your current classes are not reaching new people in your community, or that visitors have been asking about activities beyond Sunday worship. Remember this important information as you begin to form your groups. Remember the comments about why current programs aren't working. Listen for creative ideas from the people with whom you are hoping to connect.

For example, one unexpected outcome we found as a result of listening to our community was that people preferred meeting every other week or twice a month instead of once a week. Our people told us they longed for the connected life, but they were already so busy that one more weekly commitment seemed like a burden instead of a blessing, When we adopted the twice-a-month model, we found that it actually created space for our busy people to rest and have family time during the weeks when their small groups did not meet.

I contend that it is you, not the presenter at some conference, who is the expert in your mission field. Topics discussed in the following pages—such as when to start, how often to meet, how many people constitute a group—will ultimately be up to you and dependent on your setting. God will lead you by the Holy Spirit to do some unique things, because you have a unique context! Be willing to experiment, willing to fail, and ready to see beautiful things happen!

3

FORMING
SMALL GROUPS

3

FORMING SMALL GROUPS

We've spent some time exploring the "why" of small groups. Now let's talk about when, how, who, where, and what.

Before starting, we'll share a couple of terms that will be helpful as you consider small groups and begin setting them up. The first is coordinator. We've found that when groups make it (yes, we've had plenty that don't make it!), they include one or two people who hold things together. As in any group of people, leadership is important. Sometimes the title "group leader" is fine, but we have found coordinator to be a more helpful term. This person coordinates issues such as when the group will meet, who will provide food, who will facilitate the study time, and who will communicate prayer requests. Note that this leader does not personally handle all those activities; instead, the person coordinates those activities. Whatever the person is called, the important thing is to have someone who takes charge and is in charge. All healthy, thriving groups have a clear coordinator or two holding things together.

The other term is coach. Since small groups are a vital part of discipling adults, we make sure that each group is assigned someone with small group experience to provide leadership and a connection to the church. At Providence Church that person is called a coach. The coach leads the first two sessions of the group and then steps back, stays connected, and offers help and encouragement to the small group.

When Providence Church first began our small group ministry, there were two small groups. Rachel Armstrong started these groups and was easily able to serve as a coach for both. Rachel started a third small group a few months later and then a fourth soon after. Eventually, as the growing number of groups demanded more time and attention, the volunteer assignment became a part-time position on the church staff. This model was sustainable for several years until the growth of small groups necessitated that the staff member, in turn, recruit volunteers who had shown leadership ability in their own small groups to serve as coaches for other new groups.

Currently, Providence Church has a paid staff member who leads a team of ten coaches. Each coach handles an average of four groups, and these coaches are available to assist with new groups as needed.

Whatever the size of your small group ministry, we strongly recommend that there be a coach or point person to whom groups can turn for help with a wide range of issues, whether in choosing study materials or navigating changes and problems that arise. Besides helping with issues, the coach also keeps the group accountable to each other and to the church.

When?

There are more ideal and less ideal times to start new groups. We have found that, at our church, two times of year seem to work best. Remember that this is contextual, but it may be helpful for you in considering the right time to start. For us, the best time to start groups is in January. People begin the year full of resolve and ready to pursue what is important. Another time that works well is August/September, at the beginning of the school year. Though we welcome people into small groups throughout the year, we have found that these two times give us a "critical mass" of interested people to start new groups.

By critical mass, we mean twelve to sixteen people. A group with twelve to sixteen adults, figuring in the absences that naturally occur, will be big enough to have meaningful discussion at every session.

Over the years we have found that groups starting smaller than this have had a hard time surviving. For example, you may have six people who are eager to begin, with the intention of adding more people to the group as soon as possible. No matter how excited the six people are, life happens; and when two of those people miss a session due to illness, travel, kids' activities, or work, it will leave just four people, which will not feel like a good size for the group. It will put too much pressure on those four people, and likely at the group session they will just chat instead of doing any type of study or prayer. If this becomes a pattern, the group will not make it. Most people are not willing to carve out time from a demanding schedule just for chatting with three other people. If the group is not offering a substantial experience—a good mix of study, prayer, and fellowship—then it is unlikely to last long enough for others to be added.

One advantage of beginning groups in January and August/September is that you can get in some good sessions before hitting two busy times of the year—summer and the holidays. If a group begins meeting in May, they may not have time to bond before family vacations scatter everyone in many directions. Similarly, if a group begins in November they may struggle to keep attendance strong during Thanksgiving, Christmas, and New Year's. It is really helpful for a new group to hold at least four sessions before having these major breaks.

We have actually encouraged our small groups to take breaks from their regular meeting schedule during summer and the holidays. During the months of June and July (for us the two months of summer break from school), a group that has had great momentum can begin to feel discouraged if their attendance suffers. We have found it better for the small group to plan one social gathering during each summer month for those who can attend and then come back to their regular schedules in mid-August or September. We also encourage groups to meet once in December and then have a Christmas party, so they don't face the same kind of discouragement if their group is unable to attend as faithfully during the holiday season.

What if you have people who want to join a small group in times other than January and August/September? There are two good options.

The first option is to find an existing small group that's not full so the new people can jump in immediately. In these cases, keep in mind that it's difficult to join an existing group, so the coach should encourage the coordinator to help the newcomers feel welcome. When the newcomers attend for the first time, the coordinator should make sure to allow them and all the group members to introduce themselves before moving on to the planned lesson.

In this scenario, there is less pressure if you let new members know they are welcome to meet with the group several times before deciding whether to join the group. If this group is not the right fit, they are welcome to visit another group or become a part of the next new group that will be formed.

The second option is to ask the interested parties if they would be willing to help you form a new small group in January or August/September, or whenever you expect to form your next small group. New people often find it very meaningful to come alongside the coach and invite others to join the new group. Having a hand in the process of creating a group gives meaning to the time when they will be waiting for the group to begin.

How?

You should keep the idea of small groups in front of your church members and attenders as frequently as possible. It's helpful, for example, if those who speak on Sunday mornings mention their small groups and share about great things happening in other small groups. This creates a culture in which small group membership is the norm. When an announcement is made about a service opportunity, the person making the announcement can suggest that small groups sign up to do this together. All these references will pique the interest of those who are not yet involved in a small group.

When the two prime seasons for starting small groups roll around—January and August/September—there should be invitations to join small groups at every turn. On Sunday morning, if you have the capability, show a quick video about your small groups, or allow time for a quick testimony from a church member about what the small group has meant to her or him. Insert a card in the bulletin that can be filled out and turned in after the service if people are interested in joining a small group. Put a table in the lobby with an informed person who can collect the cards and give information.

If your church sends out e-mails, send one around this time of year explaining the opportunity to join a group, and encourage people to respond by e-mail or by following a link. If you have a website, post prominently a form that allows people to express interest in joining a small group year-round.

In the appendix of this book you'll find an example of the signup form we use at Providence, in a document called "Small Group Application." Your cards and forms might look different, depending on the type of groups you are forming. We will further discuss the various types of groups in the next section.

Even if the church is not yet ready to form a new group or groups, it's important that you respond in a timely manner to people who sign up. Let them know how happy you are that they are interested. Tell them that you'll be matching people with the groups that best fit their needs and that you'll give them more information as soon as possible.

Once you have a critical mass of people who have expressed interest, you'll be ready to form small groups.

Who?

How do you decide who should be in a small group? There are a number of ways to group people, and some of them are described below. At Providence Church, we have used all these methods at different points in time. All can be effective, so you must consider your context to decide which one or ones would be a good fit for your congregation.

Life Stage

Instead of using age as a determining factor, we have found that life stage is generally a better predictor of commonalities among group members. If you use this model, you might find your groups divided into categories such as these: college/early career; young singles or couples; parents of young children, of elementary school children, of youth; empty nesters, and so on.

There are two specific benefits to this model. The first benefit is controlling the cost of childcare. Providence Church determined early on that our small groups were the primary way that we would disciple our adults. We decided that this ministry was so important that the church would provide childcare for the small groups so that parents could attend without having the task or financial burden of finding a sitter. As will be discussed later in the book, we have found it necessary to pay our sitters well in order to retain quality sitters who will show up on time and give great care to our children. Since this commitment is paid by the church, it has been helpful to organize small groups by the children's age, for efficiency of childcare.

The second benefit is that people who are in a similar life stage are able to connect over the joys and struggles common to that season of life and to offer one another encouragement and support. When choosing study material, an intergenerational group will not be likely to choose one about parenting, but a small group based on life stage has that freedom. Finding service opportunities and fun activities for the group to do outside the regular sessions can be easier for groups based around life stage as well. Many people are looking for Christian friends to do life with and can more easily find them in a small group if the people are selected by life stage.

In addition to these benefits, I must caution you that there are drawbacks to the model as well. One drawback is that there will always be people who don't fit neatly into one category. Maybe a couple is in a second marriage, and they have teens from their first marriages but a baby from this one. Or perhaps one spouse wants to attend a small group but the partner doesn't; the person attending might feel uncomfortable in a group of married couples, and yet the person needs a group that offers childcare.

Situations such as these can be managed by good coaching at the outset. Don't label the groups strictly by life stage, so there will be room for people who don't match in every way. Single people can still be welcomed into a group that is mostly married couples as long as the group coordinator is encouraged to show sensitivity by not allowing a marriage study to be chosen for this group.

Intergenerational

People of all ages and life stages make up the body of Christ. We know that the church functions most effectively when we have older Christians sharing wisdom with younger Christians and when more settled believers are stirred up by the passion of a new generation. It can be a wonderful thing to throw all who are interested into a room together and watch community happen.

Many people live far away from their biological families and welcome an opportunity to have people of a different generation play the role of a "surrogate grandchild" or "surrogate parent." We have seen powerful connections happen in these groups. A younger small group member can invite an older member to Grandparent's Day at school for the child whose grandmother lives across the country. An older couple whose children live in another state are blessed to have kids from their small group stopping by to trick-or-treat and show off their costumes.

The other great benefit to this model is that it's easier to find a place for everyone. If you are the person trying to start groups, this model makes your job much easier. It doesn't matter if you are married or single, attend alone or with a spouse, have children or don't, are retired or still working. Everyone fits because they all share the desire to go deeper in Christian community.

There are two main negatives for this model. The first is that the church will likely need to provide sitters for every small group. This can be financially hard on the church, possibly more than doubling the budget for small group sitters. It can also be difficult to find enough sitters to staff this many small groups. The second drawback is that, in our experience, people do not automatically see the desirability of these types of groups. We consistently see group members expressing a preference for groups based on life stage. Parents, for example, seem to put a premium on their kids having other kids in the group to befriend. This has practical benefits, as a busy family is more likely to attend a small group when the kids are eager to play with their friends.

Geographic

Another way to form groups is based on where people live. Most people are more likely to attend a small group that does not require them driving a great distance. We have a few small groups like this at Providence Church, and frequently they are intergenerational. Most neighborhoods are full of people in different life stages, so when you start a group in that neighborhood or on that side of town, you will likely get an intergenerational group.

Geographic groups can also be based on life stage. There is a retirement community near our church for those over age fifty-five. Obviously, these people can get to one another's homes easily and have a group based on life stage.

One positive aspect of the geographic small group is that you can intentionally start the group on the smaller side—perhaps twelve people—with the intention of inviting a few neighbors to join them. It's a great outreach opportunity.

The most important thing is to remain flexible. You don't need to adhere strictly to just one of these grouping methods. You are the best judge of your context and your people. You might have all three types of groups within your church.

We find that one factor trumps all others, and that's the calendar. You need people who can all meet on Tuesday night at 6:00 p.m., or on Sunday after church for lunch, or whenever that window of opportunity dictates. After all, if you can't find a meeting time that works for everyone, then it doesn't matter how perfectly their geography or life stages match.

Where?

Our first preference is for small groups to meet in members' homes, as described in Acts 2. When we started small groups at Providence Church, we were meeting at a school on Sunday and did not have a building to use during the week, but we found that limitation was a blessing in disguise. Meeting in homes seemed to create a closer feeling of connection than meeting at church or in a restaurant—it feels like friends coming over for a visit.

Ideally, multiple group members will share the responsibility of hosting. It is no small thing to prepare your home for visitors in an act of Christian hospitality. We have had many people say when a small group is formed that they would be happy to host every time, but in our experience this eventually leads to burnout. In any case, even if the host doesn't burn out, other group members are not able to share in the group's ownership and responsibility in the same way.

Houses or apartments don't have to be enormous to accommodate a small group. Group members are usually very flexible and don't mind if the dining table doesn't fit everyone, or if people must use folding chairs in the living room. The only issue that eliminates the homes of some willing hosts is if childcare is needed and they do not have a suitable space for it. Groups that have children will generally need one room for the adults, usually the living room, and another room for the sitters and kids, often a den or bonus room.

It has been our experience that meeting in homes has great power, but there are times when this simply will not work. We have some early morning groups that would rather meet at a coffee shop than invade someone's home at 6:00 a.m. We have a group of young adults who all live in small apartments, so they use a larger room at church. We have another small group for parents of youth that meets at the church during the Sunday night youth meeting. Use your best judgment for each group in this regard.

What Is Needed?

To have a successful small group, several roles must be filled. We've already mentioned the role of coach, to act as a liaison to the church; in addition, groups will need the following:

- Hosts: As many homes as possible should be used in a rotation.
- Facilitators: We have found that the word teacher or leader does not create the atmosphere we're looking for. Unlike a teacher or leader, a facilitator is not expected to have all the

answers or to have the final say on any issues. A facilitator will guide the conversation and welcome other people to participate in the discussion. Also, the role of facilitator can be passed around, so people can take turns. Most studies come with a leader guide or suggested discussion questions, so facilitators don't need to plan lessons on their own.

- Food providers: As mentioned before, we strongly believe that connection happens more naturally around a shared meal or at least a shared snack. Ideally, over time every member contributes food in some way. Some groups plan for each person to bring part of a meal, creating a potluck. Other groups prefer to take turns signing up for various parts of the meal. As we seek to find balance between study and community, food is a great way to connect and relax together.

- Coordinator: As described previously, small groups work best when each member in the group feels ownership and contributes in some way, but it is still necessary to have one person who takes ultimate responsibility for the group. We have called this person the coordinator. (We do not use the term small group leader, because we prefer that the person coordinate group efforts rather than trying to do all the work.) Here is a summary of what a coordinator would take responsibility for:

  o Several days before each small group session, send an e-mail (or whatever communication form the group chooses) to remind members of location, facilitator, food plans, and what will be discussed. If needed, attach any documents that will be used for discussion.

  o Record prayer requests in a group journal. Send a communication to the group about prayer requests shared at each session.

  o E-mail group attendance to the coach (if applicable).

  o Communicate to the coach any questions or needs that arise within the group.

o   If the group needs childcare, communicate with the childcare coordinator regarding dates of sessions and locations. If the group must cancel or change locations for any reason, keep the childcare coordinator in the loop.

o   Before each semester begins, create a signup sheet for the group. Depending on how the group decides to do food, the signup sheet will vary; however, possible columns may include: host home, facilitator, main dish, sides, dessert, and drinks.

o   In preparation for each semester, find out what the group would like to study. If the group wants to do a published study, communicate that choice to the coach.

o   Collect any money the group is paying toward the cost of a study and turn it in to the coach or church office staff.

o   Consider organizing summer and holiday gatherings or enlisting others in the group to help with this responsibility.

Again, all these responsibilities can be shared within the group, but it's important for one person to take ownership ultimately for seeing the group thrive.

4

THE FIRST TWO SESSIONS

4

THE FIRST TWO SESSIONS

We feel it's important to get all our small groups started in the same way and with the same information, so that the vision will be clear and each member will understand what the commitment to a small group means. For this reason, the first two sessions are handled by the group's coach. We created a curriculum that coaches use for these two sessions, which equips the group to begin meeting on their own by the third session.

First Session

In the first session, there's a strong emphasis on getting to know one another and casting the vision for what a small group looks like. We want this first session to be as stress-free and welcoming as possible, so Providence Church provides dinner, and all that's required of the members is to show up. We also provide name tags to help people begin learning each other's names. After eating, we send any kids off with the sitters, and the adults gather together.

The content and format for this first session are described in two documents found in the appendix of this book: "Session 1 Leader Guide" and "Session 1 Participant Guide."

The gathering begins with the coach offering words of welcome and an opening prayer. The coach then begins a simple exercise for people to get to know each other. Each person is encouraged to share their name, a little bit about themselves, and how they connected with the church. The coach models this process by being the first one to share, showing that quite a bit can be shared in just a couple of minutes. As people share, we encourage group members to write down one other's names and something about each person, to help them remember people the next time they gather.

The coach then leads the group through a reading of Acts 2:42-47 as a way of thinking about why a small group would and should be formed. There is then guided discussion around the passage of Scripture, which provides background about why we are doing small groups while also modeling a facilitated Bible study.

The next part of the conversation deals with what the small group will do. The four components described in the Acts 2 passage—Bible study, fellowship, breaking of bread, and prayer—are put into more practical terms concerning how this small group can live out their faith biblically.

There is then time spent on how small groups are a safe place to learn about Christ. We have found that many of our people are hungering to know more about what it means to live as a Christian but feel intimidated or overwhelmed when thinking about how one can actually do this. Here the small group coach gives some instruction about the variety of studies that can be selected and used in the coming weeks. Group members are assured that each week there will be a designated facilitator and that no one will ever be called upon to talk or pray without wanting to. Most groups are composed of a mix of believers in a variety of spiritual stages.

Led by the coach, participants then discuss how small groups provide a place where members can practice living for Christ—that is, in the group they won't just learn about Christ; they will live out their faith in Christ. This will be done in caring for the other group members and ultimately, as the group becomes a launchpad for participation and leadership, in serving the larger church community.

The first session concludes with the coach sharing some information about her or his role as coach to the group, letting all group members know that the coach is available for questions and concerns.

After walking through this curriculum, each person or couple is given a questionnaire to fill out, asking what roles they would like to play in the group and what they are interested in studying. At the end of the session, the coach and small group members plan for the next session. They decide who will host and who will bring food. A sample form can be found in the appendix of this book, in the document called "Questionnaire."

Between the first and second sessions, the questionnaires will be used to create a roster and suggested plan for the small group. The roster aids the group in communicating, and the suggested plan models for the group how to take the member information and map out a semester or year for the small group. (The plan will, of course, need to be changed during the year due to sickness and travel, but it saves time to have an initial plan in place.)

Making the roster and creating the plan will serve as a model for the coordinator, showing how to live into the new role. The roster will be shared with the group at the second session, and the suggested plan will be explained. The members can pass the plan around and sign up for food items they would like to contribute at each session.

An e-mail will be sent to the group a few days before the next session as a reminder.

Second Session

The content and format for the second session are described in two documents found in the appendix of this book: "Session 2 Leader Guide" and "Session 2 Participant Guide."

In this second session, the coach will still be facilitating as we reiterate the information from the first session and accomplish two more goals: (1) for the coach to model what good facilitation looks like, and (2) for the group members to begin defining for themselves what they hope to get from the group and what they will commit to do in order to get those outcomes.

To help achieve this second goal, the coach offers members an opportunity to sign a group covenant. You can see a sample in the appendix of this book, in the document called "Covenant." We believe that the items listed in this sample covenant are essential in a healthy small group. Members are asked to commit to living out this covenant for a period of one year. The importance of the covenant will be further discussed in a subsequent section.

In the time since the first session, the coach has used the group's questionnaires to develop a roster and a suggested plan. At the second session, the coach distributes the roster and suggested plan. The members are given an opportunity to sign up for contributing to food needs at future sessions. Following that, the coach helps the group pick out a study to use for the next few sessions while they continue to connect.

Our suggestion for new groups is to begin with a study that does not represent a huge commitment. For example, don't jump in to a thirty-two-week study that has lots of homework. Find something that is stand-alone in nature, can be completed in no more than four to six weeks, and does not require homework.

We also suggest that new groups initially avoid studies on issues that are politically or culturally divisive. The time might come when such a study will be appropriate for your group, but volatile subject matter is probably better handled after group members have gotten to know one another.

One popular option for new groups at Providence is to base the first study on the current sermon series. If it's within your church's capabilities to write a discussion guide taking the sermon to a deeper or more practical level, this can provide a great common ground for your members. We have provided an example in the appendix, in a document called "Sermon Discussion Guide." In addition, you can follow this link to see all of Providence Church's sermon discussion guides: https://prov.church/messages/.

Third Session and Beyond

Once a group reaches the third session, the coach steps back to assume the role of cheerleader, and the group begins to take ownership for itself. This role works best if the coach has helped as many group members as possible to contribute and share ownership. By this time, members have signed up to share in hosting, facilitating, providing food, and coordinating.

Beginning with the third session, the coach checks in monthly with the current group coordinator via text, e-mail, or phone to see how things are going, to offer encouragement and prayer support, and to make sure attendance records have been submitted.

Later, as the first-year anniversary of the group approaches, we suggest that the coach e-mail the group to help them reflect on their experience and take stock of what has been accomplished. At this time the coach will offer the members a chance to recommit to the small group covenant or to choose to step away.

Providence Church offers a gathering for small group coordinators on a yearly basis to encourage them, educate them about best small group practices, and thank them for serving in this important role.

5

OVERSEEING
SMALL GROUPS

5

OVERSEEING SMALL GROUPS

During the first year and beyond, the coach will help the small group coordinator or coordinators monitor and assess how the group is doing. One simple but effective way to do this is by checking attendance.

Our groups are asked to send the coach an e-mail after each session with attendance information. The coach tracks this information because it's a good indicator of the group's health, and it also lets the church know if the small group model is achieving our goals.

If we connect a person to a small group, we might assume we are successfully walking the road of discipleship with that person. However, if the attendance records show that the person only attended one session, we realize that something isn't working. The coach can then reach out to that individual and find out if another group or a different meeting time might be a better fit. Since the coach is outside the small group, this individual might be willing to share things about the group that otherwise would never have been mentioned.

The Life Cycle of Groups

All small groups have a life cycle. Each group experiences a birth, a life, and a death. From the beginning it's important for the coach to discuss this issue with the group, making it clear that there isn't one ideal life span for every group.

Currently, for example, the two original small groups of Providence Church still meet regularly as they have done for nine years. Yet during that nine-year period, the church has seen many other groups form and then dissolve, with some groups lasting for as little as one year. Groups that only meet for a short season still have value and a purpose, and it's important to honor those groups when the time comes for them to end.

One effective way of monitoring group health and status is through the yearly covenant that is introduced in the second group session. In the covenant, the new group commits to meet together for one year. At the end of that year, the coach will be in contact with the group to see if all members are willing and able to commit to the covenant for another year.

This time of recommitting to the covenant allows members to step away if for any reason they don't want to remain a part of the group. If several members decide to step away, the coach can help the remaining group members explore reasons for the departures and consider making changes, if necessary. The coach can help group members decide whether they want to continue meeting and, if they do, whether they would like to welcome new members.

Alternatively, the group might decide that it has served its purpose and should stop meeting. In such a case, the coach can encourage the group to have one last session, at which members are able to share what they have meant to one another, and what they have gained from the group, and offer each other a blessing as each individual moves forward.

When a group dissolves, members often feel a sense of disappointment. Most people would love to be a part of a group that meets together for years and years, so the coach has an important role in validating the work of the group, no matter how short or how long it has lasted. It's God's good plan that each of them will move on to new places of connection and community. The coach can follow up with individual members to help them find a new group when they are ready.

An unhealthy way for a group to dissolve is for one person in the group, usually the coordinator, to decide that the group should stop meeting. This might happen if the coordinator is feeling overworked or frustrated by lower attendance. The coach can help avoid this outcome by staying in communication with group coordinators and helping them through frustrations. If the coach acknowledges from the beginning that all groups end at some point and assures the group that they will have guidance along the way, this type of unhealthy ending is less likely to occur.

Group Size

Some churches use a model of growth in which members of a small group are encouraged to invite friends to the group, and then the group divides into two groups when it becomes necessary. There are certainly merits to this method of forming new groups, but it's not the method we've used at Providence. We've opted to start new groups for new people instead of dividing existing groups. It's been our observation that, in the process of dividing, a group can sometimes lose the spark that made it dynamic to begin with.

We start our small groups with a full membership of twelve to sixteen adults, so if every group member invited just one friend, the group would quickly become too large to meet in a home or to have enough time for each person to share. For that reason, when we start a new group, the coach explains that the group is beginning at the optimal size and that it would be best not to invite new members without the agreement of the group as a whole.

For a church that values welcoming people and desires to see church members sharing God's love, this directive may seem strange. Yet, at Providence we have seen the value of protecting small groups by not allowing them to become too large. When small groups are no longer small they can be good, but almost certainly they will change, and in our experience they can also become less effective.

This size limitation will sometimes lead people in a group to start another group that has room to welcome friends of theirs in. The original group members might remain as part of both groups or may eventually choose one of the groups to invest in fully.

Sometimes, of course, a group finds itself with space to welcome new members, for whatever reason. In such cases, the coach can help match the group with newcomers, or the group can recruit new members themselves. In either case, communication is the key to making this work, so the size of the group remains manageable.

How Is a Small Group Different from a Short-Term Bible Study?

We see our small groups as something different and separate from our short-term Bible study groups, although there is some overlap between the purposes of each. Each semester we offer short-term Bible studies that last four to twelve weeks. These studies are open to anyone and do not carry any commitment beyond the length of that one study. The main purpose of these groups is for people to study the Bible and go deeper in their own faith. While connection and community do occur among members of a Bible study, these outcomes are not its primary purpose, and time is not provided for relationships to grow.

In our small groups, by contrast, there is an equal emphasis on study and relationship. Small groups are intended to stay together for a longer period of time, creating a deep sense of community and of doing life together. Our small groups provide time for relationships to grow by eating together and holding social gatherings. However, time for Bible study and prayer is certainly valued, because the relationships are Christ-centered.

We realize that some people are not ready to commit to an ongoing small group, so a short-term Bible study gives them a chance to learn and grow without feeling pressure. Short-term Bible studies also give members of small groups an opportunity to study subjects of particular interest to them that might not be covered in their small group. We see great value to both models, and we use both.

CONCLUSION:
THE CONNECTED LIFE

CONCLUSION:
THE CONNECTED LIFE

Everyone's experience of small groups is different. And in all those experiences, we see Christ at work.

Allen and Brittany shared with their small group that they were moving back to Pittsburgh. A promotion had opened up near Allen's hometown, and it seemed best to move the family back to where he had always thought they would return. It was a great opportunity, but the decision was difficult. The ten years in Nashville had held a lot of firsts, some great joys, and a few deep losses. Allen and Brittany had bought their first home, had begun to raise two children, and had experienced the devastating loss of their first child. They helped start Providence Church. Tears were shed in the living room where the small group had met for three years. A going-away gift was shared. A prayer was offered. The group gathered around them, extending their hands and praying a leave-taking blessing on this family that was a part of a larger family. One afternoon recently, Allen called me from Pittsburgh. He had gone up ahead of the family to begin work while

Brittany made arrangements to sell their home in Nashville. Allen told me he was coming home. I said, "Allen, I thought you were home. You're back in Pittsburgh." He told me, "I thought so, too. But now our home is with this church." I knew what he meant. I knew what he had found, what he realized he couldn't give up: the connected life.

Marianne was one of the first who believed in the vision for our new church. She was there at our first official gathering—eighteen people in folding chairs in the Armstrong living room. I couldn't believe she had come. Marianne was the kind of lady who could get things done. She was the kind of woman you wanted on your side. She had a powerful energy and joy that would fill a room. And there she was, filling our still-unfurnished living room with that energy and joy, saying that she was in. And she was. Over the next seven years she gave her heart, time, energy, and money to our new church. She and her husband, Al, were a part of our first small group. They were faithful in attending and in serving. Then Marianne got sick. The doctors said her time was short, and it was. In her last months, she still had the same power and joy, and she continued to share it. Her small group came around her and Al as they experienced their last days together. It seemed that whenever I went to visit Marianne, someone from the group answered the door. Group members cooked meals; provided transportation for Al, who is blind; or just sat and talked with them. After Marianne died, the small group kept a promise that never had to be spoken. They would be there for Al. And they still are. They are connected in life and in death.

Randy and Donna met in a little town where they attended high school. They fell in love. Then, as often happens with high school sweethearts, they broke up, never to speak again. Or so they thought. Randy and Donna reconnected three decades later after taking different paths. They fell in love again. They began attending a new church that met in a middle school gym. They joined a small group. The small group became their family, a place of deep connection and of life. Their wedding was the first in our new church building. It was a small wedding, attended only by family and their small group. The ceremony concluded with the small group surrounding the bride and groom. The group laid hands on them and offered a prayer of blessing. I had never seen a wedding end like that, with friends embracing each other in tears, laughing, excited about what the future would hold for the couple and for the group.

Leading, forming, and sustaining small groups is hard work. It's messy at times. It requires a lot of time and a lot of prayer. It is worth it. The connected life is available to those of us who follow Jesus, and it is most richly enjoyed, I believe, in the company of a small group of people who meet around a table or in a living room to study, experience fellowship, break bread, and pray.

APPENDIX:

SAMPLE FORMS

APPENDIX:

SAMPLE FORMS

Small Group Application 71

Questionnaire 74

Covenant 75

Session 1 Leader Guide 76

Session 1 Participant Guide 82

Session 2 Leader Guide 86

Session 2 Participant Guide 89

Sermon Discussion Guide 91

Small Group Application

A Small Group is a gathering of around 15-20 people who meet twice a month (or more) for food, fellowship, Bible study, and prayer. Most groups meet in homes or coffee shops. We have groups for people of all ages and stages of life. Providence Small Groups are for anyone who wants to connect with others and grow deeper in their Christian faith.

What To Expect

Ideally, Small Groups meet in the home of one of the group members. Some of our Small Groups also meet in restaurants or other public locations. Anywhere with room!

What does a typical meeting look like?

In a Small Group, people generally take turns hosting and facilitating the discussion. Most groups meet twice a month for an hour to an hour-and-a-half (decided by the group). Although all groups are designed uniquely, a typical Small Group meeting might be:

Seeing those who feel disconnected from God and the church find hope, healing, and wholeness in Jesus Christ.

> 6:30 p.m. Food (snacks or more)
>
> 7:00 p.m. Study & discussion
>
> 7:45 p.m. Prayer
>
> 8:00 p.m. End

What happens on the weeks in-between?

On off weeks, Small Group participants may keep this time as a date night with their spouse, a special event with children, time for a good book, or a walk in the park.

What is expected of me?

We encourage everyone to participate as much as they feel comfortable. You will not be put on the spot or expected to speak or pray aloud. Volunteers who feel comfortable doing so sign up to lead the discussion or host the evening.

What about my children?

We have several Small Groups that provide childcare. Approved childcare workers from Providence Church take care of the children in a separate room in the host home. For more info on Small Groups, please email us at info@prov.church.

Ready to join a Small Group?

Please complete the form below. You may indicate which group you are interested in, or the Small Group team of coaches can assist you in finding the best fit.

Please select any that apply.

❑ Couples (20s/30s)   ❑ Parents of Youth

❑ Murfreesboro - mixed ages   ❑ Singles (20s/30s)

❑ 50Plus Singles   ❑ 50Plus Women's Daytime

Other Small Group Information

Please complete the information below. It helps us know a little bit more about the type of Small Group you are looking for and helps us align you with a Small Group if one of the new Small Groups forming above are not a good fit for you at this time.

I am available on the following days:

❑ Monday   ❑ Friday

❑ Tuesday   ❑ Saturday

❑ Wednesday   ❑ Sunday

❑ Thursday

I would be interested in a group that includes:

❑ Men ❑ Women

❑ Married Couples ❑ Parents of Babies & Toddlers

❑ Parents of Elementary Age Kids ❑ Parents of Teenagers

❑ Empty Nesters ❑ Singles

❑ Mix of Couples & Singles ❑ Age 55+

Age Range:

❑ 20s–30s ❑ 40s–50s ❑ 60s+

I prefer:

❑ Daytime ❑ Evening

Would you be willing to host a Small Group in your home?

❑ Yes ❑ No

Are you interested in coordinating a new Small Group?

❑ Yes ❑ No

Please provide any additional comments you may have.

_____

_____

_____

Name * _____

Phone * _____

Email * _____

*Required

Questionnaire

Name: _____ Contact info: _____

Are you open to hosting meetings at your home?

_____
_____
_____
_____

Are you open to facilitating discussion?

_____
_____
_____
_____

Are you interested in being the group coordinator?

_____
_____
_____
_____

What topics or studies (if any) interest you?

_____
_____
_____
_____

Anything else I should know?

_____
_____
_____
_____

Covenant

Date: _____

We covenant to…

• Pray together and for one another.

• Devote time during each meeting to study together.

• Actively participate and engage in the Small Group meeting.

• Respond to group communications and inform the group of an absence.

• Respect differences, treat each other with love.

• Keep what is shared within the Small Group confidential.

• Provide care to every member of the Small Group.

• Serve together at least twice a year.

• Review and recommit in one year.

_____

_____

_____

_____

Group Members Sign Below

_____

_____

Session 1 Leader Guide

CHECKLIST FOR THE COACH:

Name Tags

Pens

Member Questionnaire

Copies of Lesson for Participants

Copy of Lesson for Coach

Copy of Attendance Roster

To Begin the Meeting:

COACH: Open with prayer. Please note that any underlined word on this outline is a blank on their outline. They will need time to fill in the blank when you reach each one. All words in gray appear only on the Coach's Outline.

Let's begin by getting to know each other:

COACH: You will begin by explaining to the group that they should share their name, a little bit about themselves, and their Providence story. You will model this process by being the first one to share. Explain that you would like each member to write down the other members' names and something that stands out to you about them. This will help in learning names since members could go two weeks before seeing each other again. Encourage them to keep this paper so they can refer back to it until everyone's names are learned.

NAME	CHARACTERISTICS
1. _____	
2. _____	
3. _____	
4. _____	
5. _____	
6. _____	
7. _____	
8. _____	
9. _____	
10. _____	
11. _____	
12. _____	
13. _____	
14. _____	
15. _____	
16. _____	
17. _____	
18. _____	
19. _____	

Why Small Groups?

COACH: We will provide the Biblical foundation on which Small Groups have been designed and then connect that to the mission of Providence Church. Begin by reading Acts 2:42-47 and encourage the participants to follow along.

Acts 2:42-47 (NIV – New International Version)

The Fellowship of the Believers

[42] They devoted themselves to the apostles' teaching and to fellowship, to the breaking of bread and to prayer. [43] Everyone was filled with awe at the

many wonders and signs performed by the apostles. [44] All the believers were together and had everything in common. [45] They sold property and possessions to give to anyone who had need. [46] Every day they continued to meet together in the temple courts. They broke bread in their homes and ate together with glad and sincere hearts, [47] praising God and enjoying the favor of all the people. And the Lord added to their number daily those who were being saved.

COACH: Ask the participants what in this verse stands out to them. Be prepared to help guide them to things like sharing food together, that they learned together, etc. Give them time to think and share. Then, help them connect this verse with the mission of Providence.

The vision of Providence United Methodist Church is to see those who feel disconnected from God and the church find hope, healing, and wholeness in Jesus Christ. Small Groups help the church live into this vision by being a place where people can:

Seek God: Acts 2:46a – "Every day they continued to meet together in the temple courts."

Welcome People: Acts 2:44a – "All the believers were together"

Offer Christ: Acts 2:42, 46b - "They devoted themselves to the apostles' teaching and to fellowship, to the breaking of bread and to prayer…. They broke bread in their homes and ate together with glad and sincere hearts."

Respond by Serving: Acts 2:45 – "They sold property and possessions to give to anyone who had need."

COACH: Assure the participants that no one is expecting them to sell all their possessions, but we know they will support one another when there is a need, like bringing dinner after a surgery.

What will a Small Group do?

Small Groups provide a place for people to intentionally join together to actively pursue Christ through relationships, learning, living, and serving.

1. **Small groups will build Christ-centered relationships within the Church by:**
   a. Breaking bread together
   b. Socializing together
   c. Studying together
   d. Praying together and for each other

All four components are important to a healthy group and can only be achieved if everyone makes attendance as much a priority as possible.

2. **Small groups will be a safe place to learn about Christ.**
   a. Approximately an hour should be devoted to studying together. These studies may include the sermon discussion guide, published studies, or other related activity. COACH: Encourage the participants to use the discussion guides for the first few months as the group begins to get to know each other and gel. It's common ground since they are based on the sermons and require less intense preparation work, which may feel more comfortable to some participants. Show them an example of the guide.

   b. Discussion facilitation will ideally rotate between at least two members of the group. These individuals will be responsible for coming prepared to facilitate the discussion. Since they are not lecturing on a topic, these discussions will be stronger and the group will gel quicker if as many people as who feel comfortable join in on the discussions.

   c. No one will ever be called on to pray or talk.

   d. Groups may be composed of a mix of believers in a variety of spiritual stages. We believe that this is a beautiful representation of Ephesians 4:11-13 (NIV):

[11] So Christ himself gave the apostles, the prophets, the evangelists, the pastors and teachers, [12] to equip his people for works of service, so that the body of Christ may be built up [13] until we all reach unity

in the faith and in the knowledge of the Son of God and become mature, attaining to the whole measure of the fullness of Christ. COACH: Use this to encourage believers who may feel frustrated that others are not as spiritually invested as they are. Our groups have been known to be comprised of everyone from very mature believers to nonbelievers.

3. **Small Groups will provide a place where members can practice living for Christ.**

   a. The beauty of learning about Christ is so we can <u>live</u> for Christ. Participants will encourage each other to use their given gifts and talents in the church, in the community, and as the Spirit leads each individual.

   b. Even as individuals seek the Spirit's direction on their lives, Small Groups are encouraged to <u>seek</u> the Spirit's direction on their group as a whole. Some Small Groups will connect and remain a group, others may decide to multiply, and still others may need to take a break at some point. Once a year, your coach will connect with your group to check in and see where the group is so the group can be its most effective.

4. **Small Groups will serve together.**

   a. To be their most effective, participants will serve their <u>group</u> by fulfilling several roles. These will include families to host the group, facilitators to lead the lesson, a contact person who can send out email reminders, prayer requests, etc., and families to provide food which may be snacks or a meal. COACH: Distribute the questionnaire and ask the members to complete it. Remind them that being active in the group not only helps strengthen the group but will help each individual group member feel ownership and invested in the overall health of the group.

   b. One of the most important ways that you can help your Small Group is to <u>communicate</u> effectively. COACH: Responding to group communications quickly and letting your group know when and why you will have to miss is one of the most helpful things a member can do.

c. Groups will <u>actively</u> find service opportunities to engage in through the church such as Angel Tree, Easter Egg Hunt, Room in the Inn, and Worship Without Walls.

d. Individuals in the group or the group as a whole may also feel led to <u>other</u> service opportunities in the church and community. COACH: If a member of your group finds something he or she feels passionately about, the group can support that member by joining in when they can.

What is role of the Small Group Coach?

The Small Group Coach is the person who will provide support to the Small Group, be the primary point of contact, and help to resolve any problems or concerns as they arise. Though the Coach will primarily communicate with the Small Group's Contact Person, anyone is free to contact the Coach at any point. Your Small Group Coach is _____ and you can contact them by email at _____ or by phone at _____. COACH: You may want to fill in this information before making copies but this just ensures that everyone has access to sharing any concerns with you. Remember that your coach is your resource, and they are dedicated to helping your group be as healthy as possible.

Questions? Comments?

COACH: Before you leave:

— Collect the completed questionnaires

— Remind the group of the next scheduled meeting date. If time permits and you have not already decided, try to determine location of next meeting and a plan for food.

— Let them know to anticipate an email from you with the details of the next meeting, contact list of group members, etc.

— Close the group in prayer

— Assist the host family with any clean up

providence
SMALL GROUPS

Session 1 Participant Guide

Let's begin by getting to know each other:

NAME   CHARACTERISTICS

1._____

2._____

3._____

4._____

5._____

6._____

7._____

8._____

9._____

10._____

11._____

12._____

13._____

14._____

15._____

16._____

17._____

18._____

19._____

Why Small Groups?

Acts 2:42-47 (NIV – New International Version)

The Fellowship of the Believers

[42] They devoted themselves to the apostles' teaching and to fellowship, to the breaking of bread and to prayer. [43] Everyone was filled with awe at the many wonders and signs performed by the apostles. [44] All the believers were together and had everything in common. [45] They sold property and possessions to give to anyone who had need. [46] Every day they continued to meet together in the temple courts. They broke bread in their homes and ate together with glad and sincere hearts, [47] praising God and enjoying the favor of all the people. And the Lord added to their number daily those who were being saved.

The vision of Providence United Methodist Church is to see those who feel disconnected from God and the church find _____, _____, and _____ in Jesus Christ. Small Groups help the church live into this vision by being a place where people can:

_____God: Acts 2:46a – "Every day they continued to meet together in the temple courts."

_____People: Acts 2:44a – "All the believers were together"

_____Christ: Acts 2:42, 46b - "They devoted themselves to the apostles' teaching and to fellowship, to the breaking of bread and to prayer.…They broke bread in their homes and ate together with glad and sincere hearts."

_____by Serving: Acts 2:45 – "They sold property and possessions to give to anyone who had need."

What will a Small Group do?

Small Groups provide a place for people to _____ join together to actively _____ Christ through relationships, learning, living, and serving.

1. **Small Groups will build Christ-centered relationships within the Church by:**

   a. _____ bread together

   b. _____ together

   c. _____ together

   d. _____ together and for each other

All four components are important to a healthy group and can only be achieved if everyone makes attendance as much a priority as possible.

2. **Small groups will be a safe place to learn about Christ.**

   a. Approximately an hour should be devoted to _____ together. These studies may include the sermon discussion guide, published studies, or other related activity.

   b. Discussion facilitation will ideally rotate between at least _____ members of the group. These individuals will be responsible for coming prepared to facilitate the discussion. Since they are not lecturing on a topic, these discussions will be stronger and the group will gel quicker if as many people as who feel comfortable join in on the discussions.

   c. _____ will ever be called on to pray or talk.

   d. Groups may be composed of a _____ of believers in a variety of spiritual stages. We believe that this is a beautiful representation of Ephesians 4:11-13 (NIV):

[11] So Christ himself gave the apostles, the prophets, the evangelists, the pastors and teachers, [12] to equip his people for works of service, so that the body of Christ may be built up [13] until we all reach unity in the faith and in the knowledge of the Son of God and become mature, attaining to the whole measure of the fullness of Christ.

3. **Small Groups will provide a place where members can practice living for Christ.**

   a. The beauty of learning about Christ is so we can _____ for Christ. Participants will encourage each other to use their given gifts and talents in the church, in the community, and as the Spirit leads each individual.

b. Even as individuals seek the Spirit's direction on their lives, Small Groups are encouraged to _____ the Spirit's direction on their group as a whole. Some Small Groups will connect and remain a group, others may decide to multiply, and still others may need to take a break at some point. Once a year, your coach will formally connect with your group to check in and see where the group is so the group can be its most effective.

4. **Small Groups will serve together.**

a. To be their most effective, participants will serve their _____ by fulfilling several roles. These will include families to host the group, facilitators to lead the lesson, a contact person who can send out e-mail reminders, prayer requests, etc., and families to provide food which may be snacks or a meal.

b. One of the most important ways that you can help your Small Group is to _____ effectively.

c. Groups will _____ find service opportunities to engage in through the church such as Angel Tree, Easter Egg Hunt, Room in the Inn, and Worship Without Walls.

d. Individuals in the group or the group as a whole may also feel led to _____ service opportunities in the church and community.

What is role of the Small Group Coach?

The Small Group Coach is the person who will provide support to the Small Group, be the primary point of contact, and help to resolve any problems or concerns as they arise. Though the Coach will primarily communicate with the Small Group's Contact Person, anyone is free to contact the Coach at any point. Your Small Group Coach is _____, and you can contact them by email at_____or by phone at_____. Remember that your coach is your resource and they are dedicated to helping your group be as healthy as possible.

Questions? Comments?

Session 2 Leader Guide

CHECKLIST FOR THE COACH:

Name Tags

Pens

Copies of Lesson for Participants

Copy of Lesson for Coach

Sign-Up Sheet for Host Family/Facilitator/Food for upcoming Meeting Dates

Prayer Journal

Sample Sermon Discussion Guide

Copy of the church-owned curriculum spreadsheet

Covenant

COACH: Open with prayer. This meeting will focus on the need for the members to be intentional about their group. This lesson relies on discussion so the group is able to see healthy facilitation modeled for them. Remember that a good rule of thumb for a facilitator is that they should talk about 20% of the time and the group should talk about 80% of the time though that ratio may not be achieved until they have more time together. Please note that their outline has blanks after every question so you may want to give them a moment to pause and reflect so they can write some things down before you begin the discussion. As with the first lesson, any underlined words are blanks on their outline so give them a chance to fill those in as you move through the lesson. All words in red appear only on the Coach's Outline.

The purpose of our Small Group is to intentionally join together to actively pursue Christ through <u>relationships</u>, <u>learning</u>, <u>living</u>, and <u>serving</u>.

What are the things I would like to see in my life because of this Small Group? COACH: Be prepared to start the discussion with the things you were hopeful about when you started in your group and then encourage others to share.

Being intentional is a critical piece to getting the things we want out of this group.

*How can I have intentional **relationships**?* "Therefore encourage one another and build each other up, just as in fact you are doing." (1 Thessalonians 5:11) COACH: Be prepared to share some ideas like making attendance a priority, providing a social and study time at each meeting, by praying for each other, etc.

What are things we can do together to get to know each other better?

*How can I intentionally **learn**?* "I keep asking that the God of our Lord Jesus Christ, the glorious Father, may give you the Spirit of wisdom and revelation, so that you may know him better." (Ephesians 1:17) COACH: Be prepared to share some ideas like protecting the time you have for your study during the meeting as it's easy to let the social part take over the study part, coming prepared for the discussion/doing homework if working a study, etc.

What would I like to see us study together in this Small Group?

COACH: Share the sample discussion guide and that a discussion guide is available on the church website by Monday afternoon each week. Show the church-owned curriculum. Share that if the group has a different study they are interested in that they should tell their coach. The coach will order for them. The church will pay for leader guides and/or videos. The group is asked to pay for books if they are able. The church will help with books if there is a financial need.

*How can I intentionally **live** for Christ?* "For to me, to live is Christ and to die is gain." (Philippians 1:21) COACH: Be prepared to share ideas such as learning about our strengths so we can better serve Christ in the world, by being a support for each other as we seek Christ's direction, by being an encouragement for each other, etc.

*How can I intentionally **serve**?* "ever be lacking in zeal, but keep your spiritual fervor, serving the Lord." (Romans 12:11) COACH: Be prepared to share ideas about ways the group can serve together as well as be an encouragement for the individual direction members will receive.

Questions? Comments?

Give copy of covenant. Read through and explain we are committing for one year and will choose to recommit on a yearly basis. Lead in a time of prayer and commitment. Allow each member to sign the copy in the prayer journal.

COACH: Before you leave:

— Take prayer requests and explain the gift of the prayer journal from the church to get them started. You might share the story of the Small Group that reviewed 5 years of prayer requests together and how powerful it was to see all God had done.

— Remind the group of the next scheduled meeting date. You should have a host home, facilitator, and some type of food plan for the semester that the group is aware of.

— Let them know that the group will be officially transitioning to themselves but that you will still be available to provide support and answer any questions

— Close the group in prayer

— Assist the host family with any clean up

Session 2 Participant Guide

The purpose of our Small Group is to intentionally join together to actively pursue Christ through _____, _____, _____, and _____.

What are the things I would like to see in my life because of this Small Group?

_____

_____

_____

_____

Being intentional is a critical piece to getting the things we want out of this group.

How can I have intentional *relationships*? "Therefore encourage one another and build each other up, just as in fact you are doing." (1 Thessalonians 5:11)

_____

_____

_____

_____

What are things we can do together to get to know each other better?

_____

_____

_____

How can I intentionally *learn*? "I keep asking that the God of our Lord Jesus Christ, the glorious Father, may give you the Spirit of wisdom and revelation, so that you may know him better." (Ephesians 1:17)

_____

_____

_____

What would I like to see us study together in this Small Group?

_____
_____
_____

How can I intentionally *live* for Christ? "For to me, to live is Christ and to die is gain." (Philippians 1:21)

_____
_____
_____
_____

How can I intentionally *serve*? "Never be lacking in zeal, but keep your spiritual fervor, serving the Lord." (Romans 12:11)

_____
_____
_____
_____

Questions? Comments?

Sermon Discussion Guide

Curveball—Facing Unmet Expectations

Scripture: Genesis 37:1-26

¹ Jacob lived in the land where his father had stayed, the land of Canaan. ² This is the account of Jacob's family line. Joseph, a young man of seventeen, was tending the flocks with his brothers, the sons of Bilhah and the sons of Zilpah, his father's wives, and he brought their father a bad report about them.

³ Now Israel loved Joseph more than any of his other sons, because he had been born to him in his old age; and he made an ornate robe for him. ⁴ When his brothers saw that their father loved him more than any of them, they hated him and could not speak a kind word to him.

⁵ Joseph had a dream, and when he told it to his brothers, they hated him all the more. ⁶ He said to them, "Listen to this dream I had: ⁷ We were binding sheaves of grain out in the field when suddenly my sheaf rose and stood upright, while your sheaves gathered around mine and bowed down to it."

⁸ His brothers said to him, "Do you intend to reign over us? Will you actually rule us?" And they hated him all the more because of his dream and what he had said.

⁹ Then he had another dream, and he told it to his brothers. "Listen," he said, "I had another dream, and this time the sun and moon and eleven stars were bowing down to me."

¹⁰ When he told his father as well as his brothers, his father rebuked him and said, "What is this dream you had? Will your mother and I and your brothers actually come and bow down to the ground before you?"

¹¹ His brothers were jealous of him, but his father kept the matter in mind.

¹² Now his brothers had gone to graze their father's flocks near Shechem, ¹³ and Israel said to Joseph, "As you know, your brothers are grazing the flocks near Shechem. Come, I am going to send you to them." "Very well," he replied.

¹⁴ So he said to him, "Go and see if all is well with your brothers and with the flocks, and bring word back to me." Then he sent him off from the Valley of Hebron. When Joseph arrived at Shechem, ¹⁵ a man found him wandering around in the fields and asked him, "What are you looking for?"

¹⁶ He replied, "I'm looking for my brothers. Can you tell me where they are grazing their flocks?"

¹⁷ "They have moved on from here," the man answered. "I heard them say, 'Let's go to Dothan.'" So Joseph went after his brothers and found them near Dothan. ¹⁸ But they saw him in the distance, and before he reached them, they plotted to kill him.

¹⁹ "Here comes that dreamer!" they said to each other. ²⁰ "Come now, let's kill him and throw him into one of these cisterns and say that a ferocious animal devoured him. Then we'll see what comes of his dreams."

²¹ When Reuben heard this, he tried to rescue him from their hands. "Let's not take his life," he said.

²² "Don't shed any blood. Throw him into this cistern here in the wilderness, but don't lay a hand on him." Reuben said this to rescue him from them and take him back to his father.

²³ So when Joseph came to his brothers, they stripped him of his robe—the ornate robe he was wearing—

²⁴ and they took him and threw him into the cistern. The cistern was empty; there was no water in it.

²⁵ As they sat down to eat their meal, they looked up and saw a caravan of Ishmaelites coming from Gilead. Their camels were loaded with spices, balm and myrrh, and they were on their way to take them down to Egypt.

²⁶ Judah said to his brothers, "What will we gain if we kill our brother and cover up his blood? ²⁷ Come, let's sell him to the Ishmaelites and not lay our hands on him; after all, he is our brother, our own flesh and blood." His brothers agreed.

Proverbs 19:21
Many are the plans in a person's heart,
    but it is the Lord's purpose that prevails.

Summary: We began a new sermon series titled, "Curveball: When life doesn't meet your expectations" At the heart of this series is the recognition that we consistently readjust our expectations when life throws us a curveball. We studied this reality through the Biblical story of Joseph from the book of Genesis. Joseph was a dreamer, and his dreams were lofty. His dreams depicted him as a ruler over his own brothers. His dream would be realized, but not the way he or anyone else expected.

Read and Discuss

Unless otherwise noted, scriptures have been researched and referenced based on the New International Version (NIV); however other translations are perfectly acceptable to use for discussion.

Week in Review

Last week was Easter Sunday. We learned that Easter starts in a dark place where all hope seems lost (i.e., the empty tomb). Did you see light in the dark places of your life? Describe.

Introduction

Pastor Jacob shared the story of a truck driver who spoke of some of the unmet expectations and unrealized dreams of his life. Just when we think we are settling into the relationship we always wanted, or the season of life that was supposed to be easier, life often throws us a curveball. Relationships are harder than we thought. Retirement also involves caring for an aging parent. Early in his story Joseph found out that just because he had a dream, it wasn't guaranteed to be easy. He had to keep dreaming.

Engage the Scripture

Read Genesis 37:1-26
• What can you learn about Joseph's family from verses 1 and 2?
• Why was Joseph special to his father Jacob?
• What is behind the brothers hatred of Joseph?
• What motive(s) might Jacob (Israel) have had to send Joseph out to his brothers in vv. 12-14?

- How did the brothers receive Joseph in verse 18?
- The brothers stripped Joseph of his robe. Why is this significant? What did it represent?

Application

- Joseph had a vision of ruling over his brothers, but it didn't happen as he planned. What are some of the major curveballs that impacted the direction of your life? Were they positives? Negatives?
- What are some dreams that you have given up on?
- What are some dreams that have weathered a curveball or two?
- Read Proverbs 19.21. What does this verse reveal about the dreams of your heart?

Prayer

Pray together lifting up the dreams that you've shared during this time. Ask God for the strength and faith to remain focused on God's dreams for your life.